W9-AOR-894

Korematsu v. United States

Japanese-American Internment Camps

Karen Alonso

Landmark Supreme Court Cases

Enslow Publishers, Inc.

44 Fadem Road	PO Box 38
Box 699	Aldershot
Springfield, NJ 07081	Hants GU12 6BP
USA	UK

Library of Congress Cataloging-in-Publication Data

Alonso, Karen.
    Korematsu v. United States: Japanese-American internment camps / by Karen Alonso.
        p. cm. — (Landmark Supreme Court cases)
    Includes bibliographical references and index.
    Summary: Profiles the case of Fred Korematsu, who sought compensation from the
American government for his time spent in a Japanese-American internment camp
during World War II.
    ISBN 0-89490-966-5
    1. Korematsu, Fred, 1919–   —Juvenile literature. 2. Japanese Americans—
Biography—Juvenile literature. 3. Japanese Americans—Evacuation and relocation,
1942–1945— Juvenile literature. 4. World War, 1939–1945—Reparations—Juvenile
literature. [1. Korematsu, Fred, 1919– . 2. Japanese Americans—Biography.
3. Japanese Americans—Evacuation and relocation, 1942–1945. 4. World War,
1939–1945—United States. 5. World War, 1939–1945— Reparations. 6. Prejudices.]
I. Title II. Title: Korematsu versus United States. III. Series.
D769.8.A6K67   1998
323.1'1956073—DC21   97-29582
                                                              CIP
                                                              AC

Printed in the United States of America

10 9 8 7 6 5 4 3 2 1

Photo Credits: Courtesy of Janice Yen and NCRR, pp. 101, 103, 104, 106, 110;
Library of Congress, pp. 23, 26, 34, 36, 73, 82; National Archives, pp. 9, 20, 39,
41, 42, 45, 55, 61, 94.

Cover Photo: Karen Alonso

Acknowledgments

The author wishes to acknowledge the assistance and support of Manuel J. Alonso and Virginia D. McClinch. Special thanks are reserved for Janice Harumi Yen of the National Coalition for Redress and Reparations, whose generous enthusiasm for this project made possible the acquisition of many of the illustrations for this book.

Contents

Author's Note

Fred Korematsu's story begins in the troubling days that followed America's entry into World War II. At a time when Americans needed level-headed government the most, our country's leaders forced more than one hundred twelve thousand innocent citizens from their homes to live behind barbed wire. The victims were Japanese Americans, and all of this happened to them simply because of their race.

As you read about Fred Korematsu's case, you may feel that actions taken by American government officials were contradictory and confusing. At times, they were. Remember that governments are made up of people, and people often make poor choices for a variety of reasons. Fear, greed, and prejudice were some of the irrational forces behind the internment of Japanese Americans during World War II. When motives make no sense, the results that follow are often equally irrational.

None of this can ever adequately explain one of the most disgraceful events in American history. However, it is important to keep in mind the muddled mess that can result when decisions are based on prejudice and ignorance.

Introduction

Try to imagine that you are a student in California, during the spring of 1942. You are having more than the usual difficulties of a young American student in junior high school. World War II is bringing more changes into your life and the lives of your classmates than it seems possible to imagine.

The Japanese attacked Pearl Harbor in December 1941, and the United States has now entered World War II. Many of the young men in your neighborhood have already gone off to join the Army. Those who remain have registered for the draft, and could be called for duty at any time.

Your mother, sisters, and other women on your block are talking about applying for the jobs that the men who are now soldiers have left behind. To make matters worse, you have seen the American Army putting up posters in your town. The posters order certain people to leave their neighborhoods, jobs, homes, and most of their property by a particular date. The posters refer to people just like Fred Korematsu.

But they cannot really mean Fred. Fred is just a regular guy. You have seen him cutting the grass outside his home, washing his car, and going to work in the morning. Fred has also registered for the draft. Even though Fred is as ready as any of the other men in town to go to war for his country, many people have questioned his loyalty to America.

At only twenty-two years of age, Fred Korematsu has had to face many difficult problems. After Pearl Harbor was attacked, Fred was thrown out of his union because of his ancestry. As a result, he lost his job as a shipyard welder. You can hardly believe your ears when you hear that the Army put Fred under arrest because he would not leave California.

Why is this happening? Fred's parents are Japanese. Fred himself, however, was born in the United States. He is an American citizen. He never claimed any connection with Japan, and has almost no connection with its culture. In fact, Fred Korematsu can barely speak Japanese. Whenever he wants to speak to his mother, who does not understand English, Fred has to ask his older brother to translate.

Because the United States is at war with Japan, the United States Army has ordered all people of Japanese

Posters were taped to walls throughout the West Coast, announcing orders for all people of Japanese ancestry to evacuate. Directions were given about which items evacuees would be allowed to bring from their homes.

ancestry to leave the West Coast. Fred Korematsu refused to leave. The Army chose what it thought was the best way to protect America from the danger of spying by the enemy—the Japanese. They decided to remove all Japanese and Japanese Americans living on the West Coast. More than one hundred twelve thousand men, women, and children have been sent to relocation centers. About two thirds of these people are American citizens. They were not told how long they will be held. These people have not been charged with any crime. No one specific is suspected of doing anything against the United States. According to the American government, this action was justified to prevent a possible Japanese attack on the West Coast of the United States.

The evacuation order means more trouble for Fred Korematsu. It means separation from the woman he is engaged to, who is white. In an effort to stay safely in his home, he changed the name on his identification card, and even had plastic surgery on his face. Fred Korematsu stated his position in the purest possible terms: "I figured I'd lived here all my life and I was going to stay here."[1]

Three weeks after the evacuation order went into effect, a tip to the police led to Korematsu's arrest on a street corner in his hometown. (Even though Fred had risked arrest to stay with his fiancée, she would write to him later in the relocation camp, and break off the engagement.)

Fred Korematsu insisted that it was wrong to subject innocent people to this treatment without trial or any evidence of criminal behavior. He wanted the Army order that forced him out of his home and into a relocation center to be declared unconstitutional.[2]

With the nation at war, few people listened to Korematsu's demands for justice. Fred Korematsu's voice was only one among many crying out over the tragedies brought by war. In the end, Fred Korematsu would make people listen. His case would eventually be heard by the highest court in the land—the United States Supreme Court.

1

History of the Case

America began to see Japanese people arrive in large numbers after the passage of the Chinese Exclusion Act of 1882.[1] When people leave their own homeland for a new country, those people are called immigrants to their new country. Unfortunately, many people in our country did not welcome these immigrants to California. Some Americans on the West Coast felt that the new arrivals would be competition for jobs.[2] Also, many Japanese immigrants were very successful at farming areas along the West Coast, while the Americans living there had trouble growing anything. A number of Americans simply saw this as more competition in the farm industry. They did not want the new arrivals to take away any of their customers.[3]

A few political groups in this country simply did not like Japanese people coming to America. One such group called themselves the Native Sons of the Golden West.[4] This group worked hard to keep Japanese immigrants from entering the country or being able to vote once they became citizens. This group also tried to convince other Americans that the Japanese should not be allowed to become a part of America. It told white voters that the "Yellow Peril"—the increasing number of Asian immigrants—would put their lifestyle in danger. The Native Sons and other groups such as the American Federation of Labor joined several area newspapers like the *San Francisco Chronicle* to warn Americans that immigrants from Japan were becoming too numerous.[5] Their greatest complaint was that the Japanese would take jobs away from people who had been born in this country.

Racial Tension on the West Coast

Japanese immigrants had to deal with a mixture of economic, political, and racial pressures. Prejudice led American lawmakers to pass special laws that discriminated against the Japanese who came to America. Japanese immigrants could not apply for citizenship to the United States. The Naturalization Act of 1790 allowed only free white people born in other countries to apply for American citizenship. The act was changed after the Civil War to permit people of African ancestry to become Americans. However, in 1924, Congress removed all doubt about the status of Japanese immigrants. In addition to preventing any further Japanese immigration, the Naturalization Act was changed again to state specifically that Japanese-born immigrants could never become naturalized citizens. No matter how loyal they were, or how long they lived in America, these people would always be aliens, or noncitizens.

America did not change its mind about allowing Japanese immigrants to become American citizens until the 1950s. Prior to the 1950s, the only way a person of Japanese ancestry could become a citizen of the United States was to be born in the United States. Therefore, in the America that Fred Korematsu knew at the beginning of World War II, people of Japanese ancestry fell into one of two categories. One group was made up of aliens, people who were not citizens of this country, living in the United States. Those in the other group were Japanese Americans, who had citizenship because they were born on American soil. Fred Korematsu belonged to the second group.

In the West Coast states of California, Oregon, and Washington, laws that discriminated against Japanese immigrants were passed. These laws kept immigrants from becoming part of America. For instance, Japanese could not marry white citizens. They also could not use public swimming pools or live in certain neighborhoods. Although many Japanese immigrants were successful farmers, they could not own land in America. It was also against the law for them to rent a piece of land for longer than three years at a time.

When Japanese immigrants started their own businesses in America, they did so in the face of widespread racism. The Japanese-born owner of a laundry in Sunset City, California, recalled that "persecutions became intolerable. My drivers were constantly attacked on the highway, my place of business defiled by rotten eggs and fruit; windows were smashed several times."[6]

Even children had to face prejudice and discrimination. In 1905 the San Francisco School Board announced that all Japanese students, whether or not they were American citizens, had to leave their regular schools and would be placed in separate schools that had been built for them. The school board justified this action, using an old California law that allowed them to "exclude all children of filthy or vicious habits, or children suffering from contagious diseases, and also to establish separate schools for . . . the children of Mongolian and Chinese descent."[7] The school board

16

claimed that segregation (separation) was necessary to keep the minds of white children from being affected by contact with the "Mongolian race."[8] After only five months, the board decided that it would not put the new segregation rule into effect. Still, the fact that the segregation order was even passed showed how much the Japanese-American community had been separated from American life.

Kikumatsu was the father of a San Francisco student. He asked the school board to remember that all American-born people are citizens. He wondered, "How can our children become good Americans if they are not allowed to associate with other American children, to become familiar with their customs?"[9]

Yatabe was an eight-year-old Japanese American boy, affected by the same segregation order. When the school board reversed its rule, he was allowed to attend his old school with white children. In the meantime, however, Yatabe's family had moved to another part of the city. Yatabe began attending school in his new neighborhood. On enrollment day, he overheard the principal ask the school superintendent: "We have a Jap child here. Can we let him in?"[10] Many years later, he still remembered his humiliation.

Many Japanese Americans and Japanese people living in the United States had good relationships with their neighbors. However, they often had to put up with a lot of mistrust and dislike, even before the attack on Pearl Harbor. A history of unequal treatment was already in place. The stage was set for Japanese Americans to be treated differently when the United States entered World War II.

The Attack on Pearl Harbor

Relations between the United States and Japan had been strained since the late 1920s. Japanese officials resented American involvement in Asia.[11] As World War II grew closer, their differences were mostly about money, and whether trade between the two countries was fair to each nation. Before World War II began, Japanese and American ambassadors met each day, trying to work out their differences. Unfortunately, the countries made little progress at finding a peaceful settlement of their differences.

At dawn on the morning of December 7, 1941, it was clear that further peace talks were pointless. On that date, Japan attacked the United States Naval Base at Pearl Harbor, Hawaii.[12] The United States Navy suffered tremendous losses. In this single attack, the Japanese forces destroyed or damaged eight battleships, and more than two hundred airplanes. More than twenty-four hundred American servicemen and civilians were killed or missing. Thirteen hundred people were wounded.[13]

Americans were shocked and outraged by Japan's attack on Pearl Harbor. They felt that they were tricked because Japan had not made a formal declaration of war against the United States before the raid. The fact that Japan began its attack while peace talks were in progress made Americans even more angry.[14] Franklin Delano Roosevelt, the American president at the time, reflected the mood of the nation when he called the attack "a date which will live in infamy."[15] The United States Congress responded to the attack by declaring war on Japan on December 8, 1941.[16]

Not all Americans showed anger toward the Japanese Americans, however. Some Americans wrote letters to the editors of their newspapers, saying that the Japanese Americans were good citizens of the United States. However, as time went on, political groups like the Native Sons of the Golden West worked very hard to make others doubt the Japanese Americans' loyalty. Congressman John Rankin of Mississippi made one of the most general racial criticisms of the Japanese Americans. He said, "Once a Jap, always a Jap," and "You cannot . . . make him the same as a white man any more than you can reverse the laws of nature."[17] Radios and newspapers carried

Pearl Harbor was attacked by Japanese forces on the morning of December 7, 1941. Some people who would later support the internment program felt that it was "payback" for this surprise attack.

stories saying that Japanese-American people should not be trusted. A letter to the editor of the *Sacramento Bee* reflected the opinion of many other Americans that the Japanese Americans were "treacherous and barbarous by nature."[18] People are naturally fearful during wartime, and fear often causes people to listen to gossip. This combination made it easy for newspaper columns and rumors to win out against reason.

Japanese Americans were discriminated against even before Japan's attack on Pearl Harbor. However, the fact that America was now at war with Japan only made matters worse. The idea of evacuating, or removing, Japanese Americans from the West Coast was now the subject of hot debate all over America.

Henry McLemore was a popular newspaper writer during World War II. He told his readers that he was "for the immediate removal of every Japanese on the West Coast to a point deep in the interior. Herd 'em up, pack 'em off."[19] Even Earl Warren, California's attorney general, who later became a United States Supreme Court Chief Justice, added his support to those in favor of evacuation. He wrote that the "Japanese situation" would jeopardize the entire defense effort. "Unless something is done it may bring about another Pearl Harbor."[20]

A few American leaders spoke out against evacuation. Henry Morgenthau, secretary of the Treasury, urged other Americans to avoid rash decisions. Morgenthau was against taking action without proof of the disloyalty of individual Japanese Americans. He wrote in his diary: "Anybody that wants to hurt this country or injure us, put him where he can't do it, but . . . indiscriminately, no."[21]

Francis Biddle was the attorney general of the

United States when Pearl Harbor was attacked. As attorney general, Biddle would appear before the United States Supreme Court in cases that were extremely important. He also gave legal advice and opinions to the president. The attorney general knew that the alien Japanese could be evacuated and interned during wartime without violating the Constitution.[22]

However, Biddle thought that evacuating the Japanese Americans from the West Coast would be "unnecessary and unnecessarily cruel."[23] He did not agree with the idea that special measures should be taken against any American citizens, no matter where their parents were born. According to Biddle, these actions were against the protection given to all American citizens by the United States Constitution. He wrote that the constitutional rights of Japanese Americans "were the same as those of the men who were responsible for the [evacuation] program."[24] These rights entitled them to a trial if anyone in authority claimed the Japanese Americans were sympathetic to the enemy.

Biddle claimed that there was plenty of time for the Army to decide which, if any, Japanese Americans might be a threat to national security. This could be done in an orderly and legal way, by individual interviews. According to Biddle, evacuating Japanese

Francis Biddle was attorney general of the United States during World War II. He felt that the evacuation of Japanese Americans was unnecessary and cruel.

Americans from the West Coast would be illegal and wasteful.

The Nation Organizes for War

The secretary of war during World War II was Henry L. Stimson. The secretary of war had authority over the Department of War, which had the responsibility of providing the military forces needed to protect the country. As part of his responsibilities, Stimson had to select a military commander. The chosen officer would take charge of defending America's West Coast against further attacks by Japan. Stimson chose Lieutenant General John L. DeWitt for the job.

In January 1942, DeWitt opposed evacuating Japanese Americans from the West Coast. He said that "an American citizen is after all an American citizen. . . . I think we can weed the disloyal out of the loyal and lock them up, if necessary."[25] The FBI had already arrested anyone suspected of assisting the enemy. However, by February 1942, West Coast politicians, newspapers, and ordinary citizens increased their efforts to have Japanese Americans removed from their states. President Roosevelt, General DeWitt, and many others in authority responded to this pressure. They began to support an evacuation program.

It is difficult to understand why General DeWitt,

who at first opposed evacuation, changed his mind and became one of the most enthusiastic supporters of evacuation. The answer may be that DeWitt, like many other Americans, acted out of the fear of a Japanese attack on the West Coast. These fears were fed by a false alarm of an air raid on San Francisco only one night after Pearl Harbor was attacked. San Franciscans had failed to black out the city—to turn off all lights, and to cover windows—that night to prevent enemy pilots from finding America's coastline. The following day, DeWitt met with San Francisco city leaders to point out their neglect. A reporter for *Life* magazine noted that the general "almost spit with rage."[26]

On December 10, 1941, DeWitt's fears grew more intense when he received a report that twenty thousand Japanese Americans planned an armed uprising in the San Francisco area.[27] As it turned out, DeWitt's "reliable source" for this information turned out to be an FBI informant who had been fired for his "wild imaginings."[28] The report turned out to be just another unfounded rumor.

DeWitt's willingness to change his mind about evacuation might be explained by Attorney General Biddle's impressions of DeWitt. Many years after World War II, Biddle would write that DeWitt was "apt to waver under popular pressure," with a

General DeWitt (on right) is shown receiving the Oak Leaf Cluster. He supported the movement to evacuate and intern Japanese Americans during World War II. He was placed in charge of the plan's implementation.

"tendency to reflect the views of the last man to whom he talked."[29]

DeWitt did change his mind. In fact, he became one of the most outspoken supporters of the evacuation plan. Certainly DeWitt was not the only prominent American who wanted to evacuate Japanese Americans. DeWitt reflected what was gradually becoming the attitude among many Americans, wrong as it may have been.

Rumors went around that Japanese-American farmers were lighting signal fires in the fields. There were stories that these farmers planted their crops in special patterns to help Japanese fighter pilots find their targets. Two different departments of the federal government received complaints about unidentified radio signals. Anxious Americans thought these were signals to Japanese forces at sea.[30] Like the false report of a planned uprising, these stories turned out to be mere rumors.

Many Japanese Americans felt the gradual change in attitude among other Americans. One Japanese-American woman who lived during this time said that she did not feel Japanese, she felt American. Just the same, she became worried after Pearl Harbor. She recalled that the newspapers were "agitating and printing all those stories all the time. And people were getting angrier. You heard that people were getting their houses burned down."[31]

Executive Order 9066

Although there were some important victories for the Japanese empire early in the war, Japan seemed to be losing its foothold. In spite of this fact, President Roosevelt was convinced that the United States had to protect itself from invasion by the Japanese. Also, Roosevelt wanted to protect America from spying by the enemy. He was concerned about sabotage—that spies would deliberately destroy things important to the war effort like railroads, electricity plants, and factories.[32] DeWitt agreed with the president. However, DeWitt even went so far as to claim that Japanese Americans were loyal to the Japanese emperor. His theory was that disloyal people would do anything to help the Japanese win the war against the Americans. General DeWitt claimed that the "Japanese race is an enemy race."[33] This might have made it easier for him to accept the idea that all people of Japanese ancestry living in America were possible threats to the country's security.

On February 14, 1942, General DeWitt sent his report of final recommendations to the secretary of war. This report requested permission from the president to remove all enemy aliens and people of Japanese ancestry from the West Coast.[34] Many of his statements in the report were strange and confusing. For instance, DeWitt said that the very fact that no sabotage had yet taken place was proof that it would soon happen.[35] The final recommendations also gave a brief suggestion of a plan to move all the people involved.[36] This part of the program was called the evacuation portion of DeWitt's plan.

DeWitt suggested in his report that camps should be prepared for the evacuated people. At first, the camps were meant to be only temporary places. Evacuated Japanese Americans would live there only as long as it took to relocate them. However, when DeWitt's program started, the people sent to the camps had to stay there under military guard. This part of the program was called internment. ("Internment" means being put into prison.)

To support his plan, DeWitt claimed that there was no reason to believe that Japanese Americans would not turn against this nation when the final test of loyalty came.[37] General DeWitt also wrote that there were indications that some Japanese Americans were becoming organized. They were supposedly ready to attack when the time was right.[38]

Even though it now seemed clear that American

forces could easily protect American shores, President Roosevelt decided to put DeWitt's plan into effect. President Roosevelt signed a special order on February 19, 1942. Executive Order 9066 gave the military commander the power to select certain parts of the West Coast, and call them military areas.[39] The military areas were parts of the West Coast where the United States government thought the Japanese might invade. They included important factories or military forts. Order 9066 gave the military commander permission to keep out any or all people he decided were a threat to security.[40] General DeWitt was named military commander on February 20, 1942.

Proclamation 1 Creates Military Areas

On March 2, 1942, General DeWitt issued Proclamation 1. This message, combined with later announcements, identified all of California, Washington, Oregon, and Arizona as military areas. They were named military areas because the Pacific Coast was "particularly subject to attack [and] attempted invasion."[41] Although it did not immediately state who would be affected by this order, the Army announced that it would soon require certain people to leave these areas.

Also at this time, the Army used other means to

protect the West Coast from a possible attack. Anyone living in America who was German, Japanese, or Italian was required to file a change of address notice if he or she wanted to move to a new home. This was because Germany, Japan, and Italy were also at war with the United States. Anyone who had ancestors from these enemy countries had to do the same thing. With this information on file, the United States government could keep track of people who might be considered enemies of America.

On March 21, 1942, President Roosevelt signed Public Law 503.[42] This new law made it a federal crime to disobey any of General DeWitt's orders.

Three days later, DeWitt started a curfew for Americans of German, Italian, and Japanese ancestry living in the military areas. These people were not allowed to leave their homes between the hours of 8 P.M. and 6 A.M. Breaking curfew meant arrest and being charged with breaking Public Law 503. Violators were put on trial in a federal court.

Executive Order 9066 did not specifically give DeWitt the power to put Japanese Americans into internment camps. However, it did allow him to "take such other steps as he . . . may deem advisable to enforce compliance with the restriction."[43] DeWitt claimed that increasing hostility toward Japanese Americans on the

West Coast made internment necessary in order to complete the evacuation.[44] DeWitt started to plan for the forced internment of Japanese Americans.

In preparation for evacuation and internment, the proclamations signed by DeWitt gradually became more strict, especially for the Japanese and Japanese Americans. On March 27, 1942, DeWitt ordered all people of Japanese ancestry, whether or not they were American citizens, not to leave the military area without permission.[45] People who left without permission faced arrest and a trial in federal court for breaking Public Law 503. Fred Korematsu's home was in San Leandro, California, well within the military area.

Evacuation

For a very short time, evacuation was on a voluntary basis. This meant that the Japanese Americans and Japanese citizens could resettle in another home. They were free to choose the location as long as it was outside the military area. Many refused to leave, and those who did leave had difficulty finding new homes. At the border between Nevada and California, voluntary evacuees were turned away by armed guards. In other communities, Japanese Americans found NO JAPS WANTED posters, and they felt menaced by the threat of mob violence.[46]

The American military, and some members of the American government, said that the Japanese Americans were a threat to national security. For that reason, other Americans felt it was not wise to let evacuees travel around the country without supervision.[47] If Japanese Americans were dangerous on the West Coast, they could do just as much damage in other parts of the country. In order to avoid violence against the Japanese Americans, and to prevent spying and sabotage, the evacuation was made mandatory. Japanese Americans, together with Japanese citizens, were placed under guard in internment camps.

The evacuation was handled gradually, on a section-by-section basis. Posters were taped up on buildings throughout the neighborhood. These notices warned persons of Japanese ancestry, both Japanese Americans and Japanese citizens, of their date for departure. A representative of each family in the Japanese population was instructed to report to a control station. Here, they would receive a family number. The number was attached to each piece of luggage carried by the members of the family who were forced to evacuate. These people reported to assembly centers where the Army gave them transportation to their new residences.

The Army ordered evacuees to bring extra clothing, sheets, dishes, and silverware for each member of the

Some evacuees felt they were supporting the war effort by cooperating with the internment program. Notice the tag on the woman's coat, which is marked with the family's number.

family. They also had to bring any other items that were necessary for the family. However, the amount of property that could be taken to the camps was limited to what family members could carry in their own hands. Anything that was too big to carry had to be put into storage, and owners had to pay for storage themselves. The Army allowed nothing to be shipped to the assembly centers. Even family pets had to be left behind.

The evacuees in Korematsu's area were told on May 3, 1942, that they would have to leave their homes by May 8, 1942.[48] This meant that they had only five days to close up and sell their businesses, homes, and property, and find storage for their possessions. They had to do this while packing and preparing to leave their homes for an unknown period of time.

Some other Americans took advantage of the Japanese Americans' need to sell quickly. One evacuee described whites as "vultures" who "swooped down on us going through our belongings offering us a fraction of their value. When we complained to them of the low price they would respond by saying, 'You can't take it with you so take it or leave it.'"[49] Another remembered that people came in droves, waiting for their turn to come to her house. She recalled being offered fifty dollars for a grand piano. "One man offered $500 for the house."[50]

Families were only allowed to bring what they could carry in their own hands. Decisions on what to bring were difficult, since evacuees usually had only several days' notice.

Besides losing personal articles, many families also lost businesses, farms, and cars. The Kawai family owned a laundry at the time of evacuation. It had to be sold "for virtually nothing."[51] The sale price was so low, the husband was able to hide the money in a bar of soap. Another woman had to sell her twenty-six-room hotel for five hundred dollars, because she only had three days' notice to sell her property.[52] Some evacuees tried to protect their property by finding a non-Japanese person to run their businesses until they returned. When they did return, many found that the business, equipment, and caretaker had all disappeared.[53]

By the date set by the Army, evacuees had to report to assembly centers. From there, they were taken to internment camps, also called relocation centers or concentration camps. (Different groups of people used different names for the camps.) All Japanese and Japanese Americans on the West Coast were required to report to the assembly centers for transportation to the relocation centers. The only exceptions made were in cases in which the move might cause a person's death. People who were very old or sick were not exempt, however. Ordinary problems surfaced during the evacuation, making the difficult situation worse. Yuri Tateishi recalled that as she was ready to board the bus to the camp, her three-year-old son broke out with the measles. In order to keep the infection from spreading to the other evacuees, a nurse told Tateishi that she would have to take the sleeping baby away. Tateishi said: "[W]hen I thought about how he might wake up and be in a strange place, with strange people, I just really broke down and cried. I cried all morning over it."[54] Mother and child were reunited three weeks later, at the Manzanar internment camp.

2

Life in the Camps

In the beginning of the evacuation program, some evacuees went to temporary camps until the government built more permanent places for them. Fred Korematsu was one of many sent to Tanforan, a center in California. This camp, and Santa Anita Racetrack, were quickly changed from racetracks into assembly centers. Korematsu described his living quarters at Tanforan: "The horse stalls we stayed in were made for horses, not human beings."[1] Margaret Takahashi recalled that the first people to arrive at Santa Anita "had to live in the stables. . . . [The stables] had a lot of fleas, and they smelled."[2]

Historians and scientists studied the camps after they closed. It was impossible to escape the fact that the places were really prisons. One critic said it was plain

A group of evacuees is lined up under guard at the Santa Anita assembly center. From there, they were taken to internment camps, where they were to stay for an indefinite period of time.

that the internment centers "were in fact concentration camps."[3] Life at the camps was difficult, but the fact that American citizens had been unjustly imprisoned made the time in camp worse.

Since the internment camps were built very quickly, they were shabbily built. With one family assigned to each room, there was little living space for the internees. William Hosokawa remembered that the buildings "looked like chicken coops. . . . There were no ceilings, so that if a baby cried 150 feet down on the other end of this long line of cubicles, the crying could be heard throughout the entire building."[4]

The government provided little to help make life bearable in the camps. Each person received one mattress and cot, and got one lightbulb for each room. Internees had to take care of their own needs with the articles brought from home. Even though the centers were only supposed to be temporary homes for the evacuees, there was no mistake about the purpose of the camps. Armed guards patrolled the barbed-wire fences. The evacuees were truly in prison.

When more permanent places were built, they were still not good enough. Jeanne Wakatsuki Houston was a young girl when she was sent to the more permanent Manzanar Relocation Center. She recalled the room her family shared. The shack Jeanne Wakatsuki lived in was made of one thickness of pine planking. "Gaps showed between the planks, and as the weeks passed and the green wood dried out, the gaps widened."[5] During the night, the cold desert wind would blow through the cracks in the building.

Many internees also complained about the lack of privacy in the camps. Japanese Americans had enjoyed their own homes and a close family life before the war.

This older gentleman is in his room at the Tanforan assembly center. Internees were each given one cot, mattress, and blanket. They received one light bulb for each room.

At the camps, they were required to eat in mess halls with hundreds of others. Even the bathrooms and showers had no dividers.

Many years later, people who had to stay in the camps described the anger and hurt feelings that came

This bleak landscape shows the Grenada relocation center. Families lived together in one room and ate in group mess halls with thousands of others. Internees complained that these conditions broke down close family life.

out of their experience. One woman said that she was made to feel like less of a person: "You cannot deport 110,000 people unless you have stopped seeing individuals. . . . My feeling . . . went something like this: you are going to be completely invisible anyway, so why not completely disappear."[6]

Some internees refused to speak about their time in the evacuation camps, even forty years after they were released. Jiro Ishihara wanted "to forgive and forget" his time in the internment camps, but the memories followed him through his life.[7] For years afterward, Ishihara and his wife, Tama, would not discuss their wartime experience, even with their own children.

"No-No" and "Yes-Yes"

One of the events that started long-lasting arguments in the camps came toward the end of the evacuation program. In an attempt to decide who among the internees might be released, the government passed out a list of questions that internees had to answer. They deeply resented two of the questions.[8] One question asked if the internee would be willing to serve in the American military if given the chance. The other question asked if the internee would give up any claim to Japanese citizenship, and loyalty to the Japanese emperor.

The two questions split the camps into different groups that argued for a very long time about how they should answer. The arguments were very intense, even among family members. Imagine how insulted you would feel if the government took you from your home, sent you to a prison, and then asked you to serve in the United States Army. Just as you might feel if asked the same question in these circumstances, about five thousand internees answered "no" to the questions. Many internees said that they would not serve in the Army. Others said that they would if the government would give them back their rights as American citizens. Those who answered "no" to the two questions were called the "no-no" group. The people who answered "yes" were called the "yes-yes" group.

People in the "no-no" group did not like to say that they would give up loyalty to the emperor because they never had been loyal to him in the first place. Some said this was a trap. If they agreed to give up loyalty to the emperor, this might suggest that they had been loyal to him until they filled out the questionnaire. Internees who were not born in the United States faced a special problem. Their birth in Japan meant that they could never become American citizens. Giving up their Japanese citizenship would leave this large group of people with no country at all to call home. Others felt that both answers should be "yes," since they felt loyal to America in spite of the way they were being treated.

Apparently, government employees who reviewed the answers to the questionnaires did not understand that some internees answered out of anger, sometimes as a form of protest. They simply saw that many internees had answered "no" to the two questions, and decided that this meant the "no-no group" was disloyal

Two young men arrive at their room in the Grenada relocation center. The units were built quickly in order to accommodate more than one hundred thousand evacuees.

to the country.[9] Besides being labeled as "disloyal," members of the "no-no" group were uprooted once again. In order to separate the "loyal" from the "disloyal," one internment center was selected for the "no-no" group. Members of this group were sent with

45

their families to the Tule Lake internment camp. Tule Lake's camp directors had to make room for the large number of arriving internees by moving their "loyal" internees to other camps. About fifteen thousand people had to move in and out of Tule Lake in order to separate the two groups.

Later, the fact that so many internees had answered "no" to those two questions would make a big difference in Fred Korematsu's case. Government attorneys would point to the results of this questionnaire to back up one of their arguments.

How Korematsu's Case Got to the Supreme Court

Korematsu was charged with breaking Public Law 503. That law made it a crime for Korematsu to stay in the military area after the Army announced that Japanese Americans had to leave. Since Korematsu knew of the evacuation order and refused to leave, he was found guilty. The judge sentenced Korematsu to a five-year probationary term. Even though he had found Korematsu guilty, the judge did not actually sentence Korematsu to any time in jail. This arrangement would last as long as Korematsu followed all laws and obeyed any special rules that the judge might set. However, the Army insisted that Korematsu was still supposed to be in an assembly center. Although the judge tried to release him, the Army took Korematsu into custody in the courthouse.

Korematsu was brought, under arrest, to the Tanforan assembly center. However, he was not held in Tanforan as punishment after being found guilty of breaking the law. The only reason Korematsu was held captive was because he was a Japanese American. Prejudice against Japanese Americans had reached its highest point.

If people believe that their case has been decided wrongly, or that the law under which they were charged conflicts with a superior law, such as the United States Constitution, they can appeal to a higher court. This is what happened in Korematsu's case. He said that DeWitt's orders and Public Law 503 were against the Constitution. On September 11, 1942, Korematsu's attorneys appealed his suspended sentence to the United States Court of Appeals for the Ninth Circuit.[10] In this way, Fred Korematsu asked the circuit court to reverse the trial court's decision and clear his record of the conviction.

The Circuit Court did not make a decision right away. Instead, it asked the United States Supreme Court to decide whether it was correct under the law to appeal a probationary sentence. Appeals can only be made from a final judgment, but Korematsu had not been sentenced to any time in jail. Therefore, his sentence raised the question of whether probation was a final judgment in his case. The Supreme Court answered that an appeal could be made from a suspended probationary sentence. Then the case went back to the Circuit Court for decision. The Circuit Court upheld Korematsu's conviction.

The United States Supreme Court is the court of last resort in our legal system. It is the highest level to which a case may be appealed. The Supreme Court does not have to hear every appeal that is made. It may only hear certain types of cases, usually involving questions about the United States Constitution. If the Court feels that it is an important enough question, it will grant *certiorari*; it will allow lawyers on both sides to present their arguments in writing. After that, the Court will hear arguments in its courtroom, on which it will make a decision. Because of the serious nature of Korematsu's claim that his civil rights had been violated, the Court agreed to hear the appeal.[11]

3

The Case for the Government

The team of lawyers representing the United States government included Edward Ennis, Ralph Fuchs, and John Burling. These men summed up the government's arguments in the *Korematsu* case in a document called a brief.

The government had won convictions of Fred Korematsu and other Japanese-American cases at trial. Edward Ennis wanted Korematsu's case dismissed, because evacuation of Japanese Americans no longer seemed necessary.[1] However, as solicitor general, Charles Fahy was in charge of deciding whether the government would drop the case against Korematsu or continue to fight the appeal. Fahy supported DeWitt's program, so Korematsu's lawyers appealed the case to the Supreme Court.

The team of lawyers who argued the government's side of the case had to show the Supreme Court why it should decide DeWitt's program was constitutional. An unconstitutional law would have to be struck down. If the Supreme Court decided that Public Law 503 was unconstitutional, Korematsu's conviction would have to be vacated, or reversed.

The government's arguments to the Supreme Court fell into four basic categories:

- Korematsu should not be allowed to challenge internment at all because he did not raise the issue at his original trial.

- Internment was not even an issue in Korematsu's case.

- Evacuation and internment were simply used as a way of keeping safety and order on the West Coast.

- The War Power Clause of the United States Constitution allows special measures in order to win a war.

The Internment Debate

The government's case included an attack on Korematsu's right to complain about the internment, the detention part of the special program for Japanese Americans. At trial, the government charged Korematsu only with being in the military area after the date set by the Army to evacuate. As a result, Korematsu did not bring up the internment part of the program at his trial. When an issue is not raised at trial, a defendant loses the right to raise it during a later appeal.

According to the government, the only issue in Korematsu's case was Korematsu's refusal to evacuate. Attorneys for the government reminded the Court that many Americans saw evacuation as an important means of guarding the country's security. That was because DeWitt had given the evacuation order during a time when the United States feared invasion by the enemy. The government argued that the internment part of DeWitt's program was nothing more than a way to make sure that the Army completed the evacuation.

The government said that it would compromise national security if Korematsu were allowed to disobey the evacuation order because of what he felt was an unconstitutional internment order. In Fred Korematsu's case, detention was only a side issue. According to the government, a side issue was not important enough to end a program necessary to the success of the war.

Separating Evacuation from Detention

The fact that DeWitt's program had several parts brought up another point in the government's case. Each part of the program required Korematsu to do a particular thing. First the law required him to leave the West Coast. Then the law required him to report to an assembly center. According to the government, these were two separate duties.

The government asked the Court to apply a legal doctrine called separability to Korematsu's case. Separability is a rule that controls legal challenges to laws that require a person to do more than one thing. Because of separability, a person charged with a crime may only attack the law based on the legality of the original charges against him. If a defendant is charged with failing to follow only one of the provisions required by the law, he may challenge only the legality of that provision. He may not challenge the legality of any of the other provisions. For example, the government could have tried Korematsu for failing to obey DeWitt's second requirement to report to an assembly center. However, the prosecutor did not include this in the original complaint. The government argued that separability should keep Korematsu from challenging the constitutionality of the detention portion of DeWitt's program.

Keeping Safety and Order

Government attorneys also argued that there was a practical side to the evacuation and detention program. Removing so many people from one area would involve a great deal of activity in a short period of time. They pointed out the benefits of the government's control over the move. With the Army in charge of the evacuation, this program could be carried out in an orderly and thoroughly controlled way. Evacuees and their belongings could be brought away from the West Coast efficiently if all moved at the same time, and all were headed to the same place.

The government also claimed that it was in the best interests of the Japanese Americans themselves to be removed from the West Coast and held in camps. They reminded the Court that evacuees had suffered hostility at the hands of racist Americans. According to the government's brief, the Army removed Japanese Americans from the West Coast in order to relieve tension and the possibility of violence in the military area.

Finally, the government's brief maintained that the need to prevent spying, and keep peace and order on the West Coast, made the Army's internment program proper under the War Power Clause of the United States Constitution.

War Power of Congress

The War Power Clause of the United States Constitution gave Congress the right to create any laws needed to win a war. This power included the right to decide who would be allowed to remain in the military areas and who should be kept out, or excluded, according to the government. The government's position was that Congress's war power allowed it to take whatever steps were necessary to win a war.

In this case, government attorneys claimed that the War Power Clause allowed DeWitt to use curfew, exclusion, and internment. They said that these steps were necessary to protect both the country and the war effort. DeWitt claimed that the one hundred twelve thousand Japanese Americans "at large" were "potential enemies." According to DeWitt, the fact that Japanese Americans lived and worked so close to aircraft factories and supply lines made the evacuation program necessary.[2] Therefore, these actions were well within the power given to Congress under the War Power Clause.

DeWitt's Final Report Reaches the Supreme Court

Along with the government's brief, the Supreme Court received a copy of DeWitt's final report, which contained many arguments in favor of the evacuation

The government claimed that the War Power Clause of the United States Constitution gave it the right to take certain measures. One of these measures forced Japanese Americans to register for evacuation from areas determined to be militarily sensitive.

and internment programs. The report listed the Army's reasons for deciding to evacuate Japanese Americans in order to protect America from spying and sabotage:

- There were reports of signaling from shore to enemy ships at sea.

- The loyal Japanese Americans could not be separated from the disloyal quickly enough.

- Many Japanese Americans lived near military areas where they could cause the most damage.

- The many Japanese organizations and schools on the West Coast might encourage loyalty to Japan.

Edward Ennis and John Burling challenged the accuracy of DeWitt's report, but because the War Department intervened, it was sent to the Supreme Court for the Justices to see while they considered Korematsu's case.

4

Fred Korematsu's Case

Fred Korematsu had a number of people making arguments on his behalf when the Supreme Court finally heard his side of the case. Wayne Collins was an attorney with the California office of the American Civil Liberties Union (ACLU) when Korematsu met him. The ACLU was formed in 1920 by Roger Nash Baldwin in order to protect the rights guaranteed to American citizens under the Bill of Rights, the first ten amendments to the United States Constitution. These civil rights include the right to a fair trial, the right to speak freely, and the right of all citizens to be treated equally under the law, regardless of race, gender, or religion. The ACLU is not concerned with whether a person charged with a crime is guilty or innocent, nor does it evaluate the political, social, or religious viewpoints of its clients. It seeks only to enforce the Constitution.[1] The ACLU does not ask for payment from those clients who cannot afford legal services.

Collins handled Korematsu's case from trial all the way through the appeals process to the Supreme Court. Wayne Collins disagreed with the other ACLU lawyers on his team, however, about the way to argue Korematsu's appeal before the Supreme Court. Eventually, this disagreement lead to Collins's separating from the ACLU in order to represent Fred Korematsu.

Charles Horsky was an attorney with the Washington, D.C., office of the ACLU. He filed a separate document with the Supreme Court called an *amicus curiae* brief. This term comes from the Latin phrase meaning "friend of the court." Friends of the court are not part of the case. They write their own briefs on behalf of someone involved in the case because they feel they have interests similar to one of the people. In this way, they can share important information with the Court. Morris Opler also wrote an *amicus* brief on behalf of the Japanese American Citizens League (JACL).

Among the three attorneys, Korematsu's appeal took a two-part approach. Collins's part covered a number of questions raised by the United States Constitution. The arguments covered in his brief were the following:

- Korematsu should not have been treated differently under the law because of his race.

- Korematsu should have had a trial to determine his loyalty before he was sent to an internment camp.

- Public Law 503 was an unconstitutional transfer of power to DeWitt.

Horsky and Opler brought up factual arguments for Korematsu that went against the government's point of view. In the ACLU's brief, Horsky argued that

- Korematsu should be able to attack the detention portion of the program.

- There was no real military necessity for evacuation and detention of Japanese Americans.

- DeWitt's orders were based on racist beliefs.

In the JACL's brief, Opler also tried to show that DeWitt's programs were based on his racist beliefs.

Equal Protection

One of the arguments Collins made was based on the constitutional guarantee of equal protection. The Fourteenth Amendment to the United States Constitution guarantees equal protection under the law to all American citizens. Race, gender, or religion should not be factors in how people are treated under the law.

The Constitution is the highest law of the land. This means that no state law can contradict any of the rights established and defined in the Constitution. Any law written for the purpose of treating one class of citizens differently from another takes away the protection that the Constitution was meant to provide. For instance, a state law that would not allow African-American people to serve on juries breaks this rule. African-American defendants have the right to a trial by a jury selected without discrimination against their race. Americans enjoy the protection of a trial by jury. A law that kept African Americans from serving on juries would keep African-American defendants from enjoying the whole benefit of the right to trial by jury.[2]

Restriction Based Only on Race

Korematsu's attorneys argued that the only reason strict rules were made for Japanese Americans was because they belonged to a different racial group. Many facts tended to show that Order 9066 and Public Law 503 were based on race. First, the laws specifically mentioned the Japanese race. Also, the prosecutor (the

Attorneys for Fred Korematsu argued that the internment program was unconstitutional because it singled out Japanese Americans for evacuation based only on their race.

person arguing for the government) needed to prove only two things in order to win a conviction: He needed to show Korematsu's race and that Korematsu was willingly in the military area after a certain date.

Equal protection of the law does not allow the government to take rights away from any racial group unless the law meets two conditions. First, there must be an extremely important reason for the law. Second, the rules that the law sets up must have nothing to do with race discrimination.

Equal protection under the law also requires that there be a connection between the special rules and what the lawmakers hope to accomplish.

Protecting the country from enemy attack is a very important goal. However, the government failed to meet the other half of the test. There was no connection between DeWitt's rules and their purpose. Korematsu's loyalty to the United States had never been questioned. Therefore, removing him from his home in California would make America no safer than it was before.

Wayne Collins claimed that Executive Order 9066, and the military orders that followed from the order, denied Korematsu equal protection under the law because of his race. He said that Executive Order 9066 violated the Constitution.

Due Process

The Fifth Amendment of the Constitution promises Americans due process under the law. Due process requires that the same rules are followed in every court case. Rules must be followed during the course of each trial, in order to protect the rights and freedoms of a defendant. This means that, before anyone's property or freedom can be taken away, the government must take special steps. The special steps in a criminal case would be to bring a person to court and charge him or her with a certain crime. Due process also includes the chance to have your arguments heard by a jury. Korematsu's attorneys argued that he and other Japanese Americans were denied the protection of due process.

It is true that Korematsu was brought to trial. However, that trial simply determined whether or not he was guilty of breaking Public Law 503 by refusing to evacuate. Fred Korematsu found himself behind barbed wire, not because he was found guilty of breaking Public Law 503, but because of his Japanese ancestry. The Army never made any attempt, by either holding a fair trial or by conducting a personal interview, to determine Korematsu's loyalty. The Army simply decided that Fred Korematsu was a potential threat to national security because he was a Japanese American.

The government ignored Korematsu's right to due process by making a decision about his loyalty without holding a fair trial.

Surprisingly, the government created the entire evacuation and internment program without any debate in Congress about whether this action was necessary. Although congressional action was not required at the time Executive Order 9066 was signed, this would change as the result of public demand many years later. The president did not even talk about the evacuation program with all the cabinet members, who were his closest advisors. None of the three branches of government made any real attempt to protect Korematsu's constitutional right to due process.

Delegation

Under the Constitution, Congress has the responsibility to pass laws. It may delegate this power, giving it to a person or group so that a specific task can be accomplished. However, Congress must give enough guidance and information to the people receiving the power. This requirement makes sure that a person or group does not create a law that is against the Constitution. Courts cannot enforce a law that is not constitutional. By passing Public Law 503, Congress was sending some of its law-making power to DeWitt.

Public Law 503 had general support in Congress, and it was passed quickly, with little discussion among the lawmakers.[3] Public Law 503 was criticized by Senator Taft of Ohio as the "sloppiest criminal law" he had seen anywhere.[4] Certainly, this law had many faults. The law did not say exactly who would decide what restrictions should be made. It did not say how anyone should be notified of the special rules.

Therefore, Korematsu's attorneys argued that Public Law 503 gave little or no guidance to DeWitt on the proper way to write a law, or the limits to observe. This meant that Public Law 503 was not a proper transfer of power. For that reason, the law should be struck down. After that, Korematsu's conviction under that law should be reversed.

The ACLU Position on Internment

The brief submitted by Charles Horsky of the ACLU answered one of the government's claims. The government argued that Korematsu lost his chance to argue about internment, or detention, because he did not raise the issue at his initial trial. However, the ACLU treated detention as the main issue in the case.

The ACLU asked the Court to look closely at DeWitt's orders to see how they combined to force Korematsu into detention. Before March 29, 1942,

Korematsu was free to come and go from the West Coast area.[5] After that date, DeWitt's orders kept Fred Korematsu from leaving his home area of San Leandro, California. Then the Army required Korematsu to report to an evacuation center by May 3. By May 9, 1942, it was a crime for Korematsu to be in the military area at all.[6]

The combination of all these orders left Fred Korematsu with no choice. After May 9, the ACLU argued, the Army had ordered him both to stay in the military area, and to leave. The only legal response Fred Korematsu could have made to this set of rules was to report to an assembly for transfer to a detention camp. Therefore, Korematsu had to choose between detention in an internment camp if he obeyed DeWitt's orders, or being sent to jail if he broke Public Law 503—the same outcome for two different situations.

Evacuated Japanese Americans went directly to internment camps. The ACLU's brief said that this process made it obvious that the evacuation part of the program could not be separated from the detention part. The ACLU argued that innocent Americans should not lose their freedom. Korematsu should be allowed to attack the detention portion of DeWitt's orders, and ask that Public Law 503 be declared unconstitutional.

No Military Necessity

The ACLU reminded the Court of many of the important facts surrounding Korematsu's case. When the police arrested Fred Korematsu, it no longer appeared to Americans that there was any danger of a Japanese invasion of the West Coast. That meant there would be no need for spies to help an attack, since it would never arrive. If this were the case, there would be no real military reason to confine Japanese Americans.

Then, the ACLU's brief attacked DeWitt's final report, which the general wrote in order to justify the evacuation program. The government based many of its actions on this report. However, the ACLU described the report as a "wholly untrustworthy document."[7] It argued that DeWitt failed to show any proof of spying on the part of Japanese Americans.[8]

The ACLU's brief also addressed DeWitt's claims that the Army could not locate the source of unidentified radio signals. These signals were supposedly made from the American shore to enemy ships at sea. DeWitt suggested that Japanese Americans were responsible for the signals. He said Japanese Americans had to be put into camps to prevent this sort of activity.[9] The ACLU countered with the fact that radio technology of the day was very efficient. Technicians could locate signals coming

67

from a specific house, and in fact, from a specific room in the house. Therefore, any signaling that may have been done could be located, and the spies easily caught. As a result, there would be no reason to keep an entire part of the West Coast's population in a detention camp.

Racist Beliefs

General DeWitt often gave his opinion that "a Jap is a Jap."[10] He thought that a person of Japanese ancestry would always be loyal to Japan, no matter how long that person lived in the United States. He said this would be true even if the person in question was American-born and a citizen.[11]

DeWitt said that even American-born people of Japanese ancestry would "turn against this nation when the final test of loyalty [came]."[12] He did not show any proof for his belief that Japanese Americans were disloyal as a group. Also, DeWitt gave no proof to support his belief that Japanese Americans were more likely than German Americans or Italian Americans to help invading enemy troops. He presented no evidence of any wrongdoing by Japanese Americans. According to the ACLU, the Order relied only on DeWitt's race-based idea that all Japanese had a tendency to commit sabotage or espionage.

JACL Joins Korematsu's Case

When the Japanese American Citizen's League (JACL) submitted an *amicus* brief, it aimed its comments mostly at DeWitt's racist statements. Morris Opler wrote the brief. By pointing out these statements, Opler hoped to prove that DeWitt's programs were set in motion by racist feelings instead of military need.

This organization's brief reminded the Court of the many newspaper stories telling of violence against Japanese Americans. The JACL charged the people in these stories with trying to drive away their competition because of greed. Then the JACL compared DeWitt and his evacuation program to the people in the newspaper. The brief suggested that DeWitt accepted the views of these people instead of "the principles of democracy because he is himself a confessed racist."[13]

The JACL said that there was no military need for the internment program. The only proven fact was DeWitt's obvious mistrust of the Japanese Americans, due to his prejudiced opinion of these Americans. Therefore, the JACL claimed, racism alone guided the American military toward the decision to evacuate and intern the Japanese Americans. Racism is never a constitutional basis for any law.

5

The Decision

After both parties in a court case submit their arguments in writing, the lawyers appear before the Justices of the Supreme Court. At that time, the Court hears oral arguments, during which the lawyers make a short presentation of the strongest arguments in their briefs. The Supreme Court heard oral arguments on the *Korematsu* case on October 11 and 12, 1944.[1] It was not until December 18, 1944, however, that the highest court in the land delivered its historic decision.[2]

Justice Black Delivers the Opinion of the Court

Justice Hugo Black gave his decision in very simple terms. He stated that the Court upheld the exclusion order. However, he seemed to limit the Court's approval of the exclusion order. He wrote that the Court found it to be constitutional at the time it was made, and at the time Fred Korematsu violated it. This confined the Court's approval of such measures to wartime.

Justice Black said that anyone who was aware of the exclusion order and violated it would be guilty of a misdemeanor under the law. He noted that Korematsu admitted that he knew of the exclusion order, but disobeyed it.

Then the Supreme Court judge wrote about the problem of having racial classifications in the exclusion order. All laws that cut back on the civil rights of a single racial group should be questioned in order to make sure that the law was not passed simply out of racism. Justice Black went on to point out that race-based laws must be studied with strict scrutiny. Under strict scrutiny, a law will be upheld only if that law is necessary to achieve an extremely important government purpose.

Justice Black wrote that hatred of another racial group would never be enough to allow such a law to stand. Even so, the majority of the Court reasoned that protecting America's West Coast was enough to withstand strict scrutiny.

Justice Black also decided that this law had a definite and close relationship to preventing espionage and sabotage. He repeated one of the military's claims; according to the Army, the curfew order was not enough to protect America from harm by spies. Then Black referred to studies made after the exclusion of Japanese Americans, using the questionnaires answered in the camps by the internees. Relying on the study that suggested that Japanese Americans were disloyal, the majority of Justices accepted the Army's judgment that evacuation was necessary.[3]

However, the Court did not use a very difficult test to decide whether evacuation was necessary. Often, judges will ask whether another, less demanding, way to deal with a problem is available. In this case, the Supreme Court did not raise this question. Also, the Court did not closely examine the Army's reasons for saying that evacuation was necessary.

Justice Black also said "hardships are part of war. . . . All citizens . . . feel the impact of war in greater or lesser measure."[4] He recognized that the exclusion and evacuation orders were not in keeping with precious American ideals of freedom. However, he noted that in times of modern warfare, the power to protect the country must be strong enough to meet the threatened danger.[5]

Justice Hugo Black wrote the Supreme Court's majority decision that held that the actions of the government in evacuating and interning Japanese Americans were constitutional.

Court Addresses Only One of Three Orders

Fred Korematsu stated that the three basic commands of the military orders combined amounted to a plot to jail Japanese Americans living on the West Coast. Briefly, those commands said that people of Japanese ancestry were (1) not allowed to leave the area, (2) required to report to assembly centers, and (3) required to go under military guard to relocation centers where they had to stay until they were released.

In the majority opinion, Justice Black admitted that there were basically three parts to the orders that applied to the Japanese Americans. However, he denied that the three orders added up to any plan to imprison Japanese Americans. Instead, Black wrote that the orders were three separate steps of a complete evacuation program. He said that each of the three orders asked Japanese Americans to do separate things.[6] Breaking any one of the three would carry an individual penalty.

Taking this position allowed Black to look only at the evacuation portion of the program. That is because the Supreme Court only answers questions that are actually in dispute. To avoid misleading people who look to Supreme Court decisions for guidance in the law, the Court refuses to make decisions on hypothetical, "what if" situations. To do so might cause people to read things into the decision. They may try to argue their side by comparing the invented facts of the Supreme Court case with their own facts. This could be misleading to people in later cases. The government charged Korematsu only with failing to evacuate. Therefore, the majority of the Court would not comment on whether or not the internment part of the program was a proper wartime measure.

Five of the other nine Supreme Court Justices agreed with Justice Black. A majority of the Justices of the Supreme Court decided that the evacuation of Japanese Americans from the West Coast was not against the Constitution under the facts of the *Korematsu* case.

Frankfurter Concurs

When the Supreme Court hands down a decision, even those Justices who vote with the majority may have different reasons for doing so. When that is the case, those Justices can write concurring opinions. Justice Felix Frankfurter wrote such an opinion to add some of his thoughts on the *Korematsu* case to the record.

Judge Military Action Within Context of War

Justice Frankfurter wrote that the war power of the government is "the power to wage war successfully."[7] Anything that is necessary to win the war should be done. With this thought as his starting point, Frankfurter wrote that any action taken under the War Power Clause must be judged in the context of war. This means that some things done during war will be unpleasant. We may even be offended by some of the government's tactics. However, we should consider the fact that the country was at war when we review the Army's methods.[8]

Frankfurter wrote that the government has the power to conduct war. The War Power Clause demands that it must do so in the best possible way. This grant of power under the Constitution is as important as any other part of the Constitution. Therefore, claiming that an action taken within the War Power Clause is unconstitutional would be the same as saying that a part of the Constitution is unconstitutional. As long as the action taken was a proper way to fight the war under the War Power Clause, Frankfurter said, the action taken by the military is constitutional.[9]

Roberts Dissents

Sometimes a Supreme Court Justice will feel strongly that the majority of the Court has made the wrong decision, or for the wrong reason. In that case, a Justice who votes against the majority opinion will write a dissenting opinion, giving reasons for disagreement.

Clear Violation of Constitutional Rights

Justice Owen Roberts wrote a very powerful dissenting opinion in the *Korematsu* case. He stated firmly that the facts around the *Korematsu* case showed a "clear violation of Constitutional rights."[10] Then Roberts reviewed the facts as he saw them. Fred Korematsu was convicted and punished for not allowing himself to be sent to a "concentration camp" only because of his ancestry, and without any inquiry into his loyalty.[11]

"Conflicting Orders" Problem Not Addressed by Majority

Justice Roberts strongly objected to the majority opinion on one important point. He disagreed with the fact that the majority treated the military control of the West Coast as three separate orders instead of one whole plan. Roberts focused on the fact that Korematsu was forbidden by military order to leave the area in which he lived. After a certain date, another military order required him to report to an assembly center. One order directly followed the other, leaving people of Japanese ancestry with no alternative but to submit to detention.

Roberts claimed that there was an obvious purpose of the combined orders. That purpose was "to drive all citizens of Japanese ancestry into Assembly Centers," or risk being charged with a crime.[12]

Justice Roberts closed his dissent by saying that usually, an unconstitutional law may be attacked on the basis of its unconstitutionality. In Korematsu's case, the situation was very different. One way or another, Fred Korematsu was expected to give up his freedom before challenging the military orders.

Murphy Dissents

Justice Francis Murphy also wrote a stirring dissent that looked at the limits of the War Power Clause. As Murphy put it, the exclusion order had fallen into "the ugly abyss of racism."[13]

War Power Should Limit the Military

Murphy agreed that military authorities who are on the scene are usually better judges of how a situation should be handled. He felt that this was particularly true during wartime. At these times, decisions of military officials should not be changed easily by those without military training or responsibilities.[14] However, Justice Murphy insisted that there should be definite limits to military judgment when there has been little or no evidence to prove its claim of necessity. Since martial law had not been declared on the West Coast, it was even more important to limit the methods used by the Army.[15]

Murphy wrote that there was a test to decide whether the government could properly take away a person's constitutional rights. That test asks only whether that action is reasonably related to a public danger. For example, the Court could have asked the Army to show that the threat of a Japanese invasion of the West Coast was very near. If they could prove that there was no time to interview individual Japanese Americans, then the government would have shown that the exclusion program was closely connected to the protection of America's western shores. Murphy thought that it should not be made too hard for the government to show the connection.[16]

Obvious Racial Discrimination

Justice Murphy felt that the exclusion order did not meet that test. He concluded that DeWitt based the exclusion order on questionable assumptions.[17] The idea that all people of Japanese ancestry, whether alien or American-born, were more likely to be spies than other groups of people was a questionable assumption at best. At worst, it was a racist assumption.

Justice Murphy was willing to agree that some people of Japanese ancestry would help the Japanese empire in its war against America. However, he wrote that these examples of individual situations should not be used to prove guilt on the part of every member of the Japanese race. To do so would be to deny the entire system of individual responsibility that is the foundation of our nation.[18]

Since the order was directed only to people of Japanese ancestry, Murphy said that it was an obvious racial discrimination, a denial of the Equal Protection Clause of the Constitution. Murphy felt that other matters were just as important. For instance, the lack of due process deprived Korematsu of the right to know the charges against him. He lost the benefit of a trial at which he could present his own side of the story.

Jackson Dissents

Justice Jackson wrote the final dissenting opinion on the *Korematsu* case. While many of his ideas appeared in the other dissenting opinions, he did make a comparison that makes the race-related portions of the exclusion order seem more clear.

His example compared three hypothetical people with Fred Korematsu:

1. a German alien enemy

2. an Italian alien enemy

3. a citizen of American-born ancestors, who had been convicted of treason, but was out of jail on parole

4. Fred Korematsu

Jackson said that if all four had been in the military area after the exclusion order took effect, only Korematsu would have violated the order by being there. The only important difference among the four is the fact that Korematsu was born of "different racial stock."[19] This distinction is forbidden under the Constitution. Justice Jackson then ended his dissent with two urgent warnings.

"Loaded Weapon" Warning

Jackson admitted that not all military orders will meet the requirements in order to make a law constitutional. Such orders must often be made quickly, using information that may not be admissible in court. The main purpose of the military is to protect the people of a society, not just the Constitution of that society. Even so, the fact that an Army's actions may be necessary does not automatically mean they are constitutional.[20]

Jackson wrote that a military order will only last as long as the war that made the order necessary. Therefore, it could do only temporary harm. However, he warned against the danger of the Supreme Court's upholding such an order. Jackson felt that to do so gives permission to practice racial discrimination whenever it becomes desirable for some reason to do so. The decision, he said, then "lies about like a loaded weapon

Justice Robert Jackson was among the minority on the Supreme Court who disagreed with the *Korematsu* decision. He said that the decision was like a loaded weapon waiting to be used.

ready for the hand of any authority" that can make some argument of an urgent need to use racist rules.[21]

Civil Courts Should Not Be Instruments of Military Policy

Justice Jackson then warned that the judicial system, or civil courts, should not be made to enforce military orders. Judges should apply only the law. If they begin to enforce military orders, he said, the courts will stop being civil courts and become "instruments of military policy."[22]

After the Decision

After the Court announced its decision, there were strong reactions on all sides. Some felt that the Supreme Court justified the decisions that the government made during the war. Others felt that the Army's actions were wrong. This second group believed the Supreme Court made the situation even worse by declaring that the evacuation program was legal.

Among the Japanese-American community, the reaction was stronger. Since their treatment during the war was based on racial differences, the *Korematsu* decision created bitterness and resentment in the Japanese-American community. The financial and emotional damage would never truly be made right. Righting the legal wrong created by this decision would take almost half a century. Long after the American people thought the *Korematsu* case had been finally decided, evidence was uncovered that would renew Fred Korematsu's hope for justice.

In the 1980s, a legal historian made the startling discovery that the defendants in several cases involving Japanese Americans did not have all the facts at hand when they presented their cases to the Supreme Court. Several people in the government had deliberately withheld evidence that may have caused the Supreme Court to make different decisions in those cases. New efforts would soon be made to clear Fred Korematsu's record. Even with this new evidence available, many questions remained open for Korematsu's attorneys. Fred Korematsu's case had gone through America's entire system of appeal. Could his case be reopened because of the new evidence? If it could, would the discovered evidence be enough to convince a judge that Korematsu's conviction should be reversed? Fred Korematsu's attorneys began seeking the answers.

6

Korematsu's Case Reopened

In 1983, Fred Korematsu's case entered an unexpected stage. Newly uncovered evidence showed that Fred Korematsu's attorneys did not have all the facts at hand when they presented their case at each stage.

The evidence showed that several agencies of the government had withheld important facts. It also showed that the Supreme Court had misleading information when it considered Korematsu's case. The courts hearing the case, including the Supreme Court, made their decisions based on inaccurate or incomplete information.[1]

Usually, once a criminal case is decided, and all appeals have been made, the decision becomes final.

However, our legal system gives us opportunities to look into a case once again. One such opportunity comes up if the facts show a very serious injustice led to a wrong decision, or if new information surfaces about a case.

This method is called a writ of *error coram nobis,* a Latin phrase meaning an error committed in the proceedings "before us." This legal proceeding asks the trial court to vacate, or cancel, its earlier decision if facts necessary to making the right decision were not before the court during the process. On January 19, 1983, Fred Korematsu's attorneys filed a motion in U.S District Court for the Northern District of California, in San Francisco, the same court where Korematsu had his trial so many years before.[2] Almost forty years after his criminal conviction, Korematsu's attorneys argued that in 1942 information had been kept from his lawyers. That prevented the trial court from reaching a proper conclusion.

Reopening Fred Korematsu's case caused the government to begin discussing the possibility of a presidential pardon for Korematsu. This government tactic was an attempt to keep a court from considering Korematsu's claim that government representatives acted improperly while preparing his case in 1944. Even though Korematsu was wrongly jailed, a presidential pardon would be like saying "we still believe you are guilty, but we forgive you." This proposal brought about strong reactions from almost everyone. The suggestion was completely unacceptable to Fred Korematsu. As Korematsu stated, "We should be the ones pardoning the government."[3]

Many opposed a pardon for Korematsu and others who were convicted of breaking the curfew and evacuation orders. Some said that the internment program was a way of getting back at the Japanese for the attack on Pearl Harbor.[4] Since these Americans felt the internment program was payback, they saw no reason to apologize to the Japanese Americans for any losses. Almost forty years later, some Americans still had trouble accepting the fact that Japanese Americans were American citizens, and that they were not spies for a foreign government.

There was also another reason that Japanese Americans found it unacceptable to accept pardons. This gave the government a way to end the whole matter without discussing constitutional questions that the case had raised. Fred Korematsu's case would finally be over. There would be no discussion by the courts, however, about the constitutionality of the evacuation and internment of Japanese Americans during World War II. Thousands of internees would never have the satisfaction of hearing a court acknowledge that DeWitt's orders were, in fact, unconstitutional.

Korematsu Returns to Court

When Fred Korematsu reopened his case, his attorneys based his arguments on actions taken by the federal government nearly forty years earlier. What the individual government officials did was complicated, and began long before Fred Korematsu's case reached the Supreme Court.

It started in 1941 with DeWitt's statement that he believed he could separate the loyal Japanese Americans from the disloyal ones. Later, DeWitt prepared a final report to the War Department. In that report, DeWitt contradicted his earlier statement by suggesting that the Japanese Americans were different from other Americans, by pointing to their close racial ties, strong traditions, and culture.[5] Because of these differences, DeWitt claimed, the loyal Japanese Americans could never be separated from the disloyal ones, no matter how much time was available.

Assistant Secretary of War John McCloy helped gather documents from different parts of the War Department. When he received his copies of the final report, McCloy noticed the difference between DeWitt's two statements. McCloy was afraid that this inconsistency would make DeWitt seem less believable.[6] Since the evacuation program was recommended and put together in large part by DeWitt, his claim that the program was a military necessity was very important to the government's case. The government could not afford to let an important part of its case be weakened by showing two different stories.

To avoid damaging its case in this way, the War Department took back all distributed copies of the final report, and changed the way it was written. The document now said that loyal and disloyal Japanese Americans could not be separated in a way that would be quick enough under the circumstances.

The War Department also improved its argument by making this change. The new version removed any statements that made DeWitt's decisions seem based on racism. McCloy took out the sentences that said it was "impossible" to separate the loyal from the disloyal Japanese Americans. The new version stated that "no ready means existed" by which loyalty could be determined.[7] By saying that "no ready means existed," the problem now appeared to be based on more practical matters. The paragraph focused on the Army's ability to question all Japanese Americans quickly enough. At the same time, the new version hid DeWitt's openly racist motive.

With that change made, the new final report was sent to the Justice Department. The War Department destroyed all records that showed that a first version existed, or that a second version took its place. The War Department also lied to the Justice Department. The Justice Department is the part of the government that prepares and argues cases in the Supreme Court. The War Department claimed that only one version of the final report ever existed.[8]

The Court never heard the fact that two versions of the final report existed. They never knew that DeWitt told two different stories about whether or not loyal and disloyal Japanese Americans could ever be separated.

If the Supreme Court had been allowed to read DeWitt's statement that it was impossible to make such a separation, no matter how much time was available, they might have reached a different decision. They could easily have decided that DeWitt's orders were based on racist assumptions instead of a reasonable review of the facts.

Suppressed Evidence

In addition to creating a second version of the final report in order to hide DeWitt's changing opinion on the loyalty of Japanese Americans, other information was kept away from the Supreme Court.

For instance, DeWitt referred to the stories that radio signals were sent from the California shore to Japanese ships at sea. These signals were supposed to help the enemy find a target on shore to attack. The Federal Bureau of Investigation (FBI), the Federal Communications Commission (FCC)—the agency that controls broadcast signals, and the Navy all looked into the rumors.

Every claim of illegal radio signals had been investigated and found to be false, but the Justice Department never gave this information to the courts. As it turned out later, DeWitt knew that the FBI investigated the reports of radio signals. He also knew that the FBI decided these harmless signals were easily explained.[9] In fact, DeWitt had this information before the Japanese Americans were evacuated.

The fact that the Supreme Court had incomplete and incorrect information made the *Korematsu* decision inaccurate. The fact that different parts of the government deliberately kept full and truthful information from the Supreme Court, however, created much more complex issues. Korematsu now had an unjust criminal conviction on his record. In order to correct this terrible injustice, Korematsu's attorneys filed a petition in Federal District Court where he was originally convicted, requesting that his case be reopened.

The request to reopen Fred Korematsu's case would be brought before Judge Marilyn Hall Patel for decision.

The Government Responds

The government answered Korematsu's petition in a very surprising way. Victor Stone, counsel for the United States government, responded with a document that was made up of only four pages. In it, the government did not oppose Korematsu's request that the conviction be vacated.

Stone did not want Judge Patel to consider Korematsu's claims that the government had acted improperly.[10] Instead, the government's attorneys wanted the Court to approve their own motion (request). This motion asked the Court to dismiss the charges against Korematsu, because they had decided not to continue the prosecution.

Judge Patel Makes Her Decision

Since the government did not want the Court ever to consider whether Korematsu's charges of government misconduct were true, this gave Judge Patel the chance to avoid looking at Korematsu's claims, in case Mr. Stone's request turned out to be proper.

Judge Patel pointed out that the legal tool the government wanted to use to dismiss the charges against Korematsu was like a *nolle prosequi*. In Latin, this means

"I am unwilling to prosecute." According to the judge, this motion should have been made before the trial started. This method would allow the government to stop prosecuting a case that it had started, but which was still in progress—not a case that had already been decided.

This motion is no longer appropriate once a criminal defendant has been through a trial, been convicted, served his sentence, and lived with the results of his conviction. Since that is exactly what happened in Fred Korematsu's case, Judge Patel denied the government's motion.

Korematsu's *Coram Nobis* Motion Granted

The government did not disagree with Korematsu's statement of the facts. Courts usually did not waste time judging the truth of facts if there is no opposition to them. However, the government never actually confessed to doing anything wrong, so the court decided to look into the facts presented by Korematsu. The judge described the government attorney's motive as an apparent effort to "put this unfortunate episode in our country's history behind us."[11]

Important information had been kept from the courts at every level during Korematsu's trial and appeal process. According to the judge, it did not matter if the ruling would have been different if the courts had all

Many people were taken from an assembly point (like the one shown here) to a relocation center, where they were forced to remain throughout much of the war.

the suppressed information at hand. The fact that Fred Korematsu did not have a fair trial because of the government's actions was a strong enough reason to grant the motion in Korematsu's favor.

The judge found enough evidence to show the court it must correct a "complete miscarriage of justice." It was also important, she said, to keep the public's confidence in the legal system. Therefore, Judge Patel ordered that Fred Korematsu's motion to set aside his forty-year-old conviction be granted.[12]

Judge Patel's order was a big step toward correcting the wrongdoing of an earlier time, but even she saw that Fred Korematsu's victory in her court that day was incomplete. The Supreme Court's *Korematsu* decision "remained on the pages of our legal and political history." Although this was unfortunately true, Patel agreed with Stone and others that the decision was "overruled in the court of history."[13] Time and history proved the *Korematsu* decision to be wrong. That was some satisfaction, even though it was never actually overruled by a new Supreme Court decision.

At the end of her decision, Judge Patel said that the true value of the *Korematsu* decision was as a warning for times of war. During such periods, we must always be especially careful to protect our constitutional rights.

7

Compensation and Apologies

The United States Army announced its decision to end the evacuation and internment programs just hours before the *Korematsu* decision was handed down by the Supreme Court. Still, the exclusion order did not formally come to an end until January 2, 1945.[1]

One by one, the camps closed and evacuees were allowed to return home in a slow but steady stream. Some white Americans welcomed their returning neighbors with open arms; others were suspicious. In some cases, the returning Japanese Americans were greeted with violence.

With the nation still at war, some returnees had to rebuild their lives in the face of hostility from other

Americans. Unfortunately, they no longer had the many possessions and resources they had left behind when they were ordered out of the military areas. Although they now had their freedom, those who had resisted the Army's orders now had criminal records. Those Japanese who had emigrated from Japan to begin again in America now had to start over a second time. All Japanese Americans had to live with the history of having been treated as threats to their communities.

Three years after the war ended, the American government began making efforts to repay the Japanese Americans for some of the money and property they had lost as a result of the evacuation and internment programs.

Early Efforts to Compensate

In 1948, Congress passed the Japanese American Evacuation Claims Act.[2] This law allowed those who were in internment camps to file claims with the federal government, asking the United States government to pay back Japanese Americans for the money or property they lost. Unfortunately, there were a lot of problems with the Claims Act. The act was passed too late to help some internees, and it did not provide relief for all the damage suffered by those who filed claims.

First, many financial papers and records were lost or

destroyed when the internees had to leave their homes. Also, by 1948, the federal government had already destroyed tax returns for the years 1939 through 1942.[3] These documents would have helped internees show the exact amount of money they lost.

In addition to the difficulty of proving their claims, internees also had to wait a very long time for their claims to be reviewed. The attorney general had to review each application personally, so the process took a long time. During the first two years, more than twenty-six thousand claims were sent to the attorney general, and only 232 were settled.[4] Obviously, the Claims Act was not very efficient. This inefficiency also surfaced when the government disagreed with a claim. When one person filed a claim for $450 under this act, the government spent over $1,000 fighting that claim.[5]

The Claims Act did not give relief for the most painful kinds of suffering experienced by the internees, however. The act did not allow payments for loss of earnings or profits, or for sale of property below its true value. Also, the act did not allow payments for any kind of emotional suffering, or for loss of freedom. Yoshio Ekimoto filed a claim under this act, because he lost his farm and other personal property. Evacuation and internment brought great suffering to all internees, but additional pain came to Ekimoto when his wife miscarried as a result of internment. He claimed $23,824 for the loss of his property, but the government paid him only $692. The Ekimoto family could never be compensated for their personal pain.[6]

The Japanese American Evacuation Claims Act failed to provide relief to the returnees in a meaningful way. As time moved on, however, the efforts to see the victims of the internment program receive justice would get results.

Presidents and Congress Take Action

In 1971, President Nixon signed a law that required action by Congress before any order like Executive Order 9066 could ever be issued again. In 1976, President Ford signed a repeal law, cancelling the law under which Fred Korematsu was convicted. Then President Ford signed another law that formally ended all power given by Executive Order 9066. Even though Ford pointed out that Executive Order 9066 was meant only to last as long as World War II, he left no confusion about the fact that this order no longer had any power.

It was the two hundredth anniversary of American independence, and President Ford used this occasion to reassure the Japanese-American community that the government was aware of the mistake it had made. He wanted to make sure all Americans learned from the experience. Ford announced that he wished all Americans to join with him in making an American promise—"that we have learned from the tragedy of that long-ago experience forever to treasure liberty and justice for each individual American, and resolve that this kind of action shall never again be repeated."[7]

Reparations Act of 1988

Many Americans felt that the matter of the Japanese-American internment camps was still not settled. Many said that the American government had not done all it could to heal the open wounds left by the experience in the camps.[8]

The Japanese American Citizens League (JACL) first began talking about the idea of asking Congress to make reparation payments to the people who had been in the camps. A large sum of money could be paid to those who had been wronged. It was meant to show that the United States government admitted responsibility for doing something wrong.

Japanese Americans supported the idea. A survey taken in the Japanese-American community showed that 94 percent of the people who answered said that the government should make some sort of reparation payment.[9]

The Japanese-American community encouraged redress payments to those who had been held in the camps. In 1984, activism drives such as this one encouraged supporters to write letters to Congress.

Supporters of the reparation payments gave several reasons for their position. John Tateishi was three and a half years old when he was sent to internment camps. He said it would be a way of making sure that nothing like this would "ever happen again."[10] Supporters looked at the money as a sign that the government admitted its actions were wrong. Norman Mineta, who was interned as a child, answered those who said "liberty is priceless," and "you cannot put a price on

101

freedom." "That's an easy statement when you have your freedom," Mineta said. Having had his rights "ripped away" from him, Norman Mineta felt he was "absolutely" entitled to compensation.[11]

Some Japanese Americans felt ashamed about being put in jail during the war. Jeanne Wakatsuki Houston remembers wondering as a child why she was in a camp. "Then your mother says, 'Because you are Japanese.' It was something to be ashamed of."[12] They felt that somehow there must be something wrong with them, or that they must have deserved the treatment they received.[13] Having the government pay them the money would be a sign to them that they did nothing wrong.

However, not all Japanese Americans agreed that reparation payments should be made. Senator Hayakawa of California argued that it was a way of "hustling" money from a government that could be made to feel guilty.[14] They were afraid that the payments might only make other Americans resentful, and reawaken mistrust against the Japanese-American community. Also, this group did not think it would be likely that the Congress would want to spend a large sum of money this way.[15]

When the bill was presented to Congress, it caused a great deal of commotion. President Reagan threatened

Though some Japanese Americans have tried to forget about the indignities of the internment camps, others such as these marchers have tried to increase public awareness of what took place during World War II.

Fred Korematsu responds to applause after being introduced among the audience members at a 1988 victory gathering celebrating passage of the reparations bill.

to veto the bill because of the estimated $1 billion it would cost. Reagan said that it was not proper to "pass judgment on those who may have made mistakes while the country was struggling for survival." He felt that we must simply recognize that the internment program was "just a mistake."[16] Senator Jesse Helms of North Carolina did not want the bill to pass until the Japanese government first took action. He wanted Japan to make payments to the families of Americans killed in the attack on Pearl Harbor.[17]

Despite some opposition, the bill was signed on August 10, 1988.[18] Included in the bill were several admissions. The government admitted that a "grave injustice" had been committed and that the action had been taken without security reasons that were strong enough. There was also no evidence of spying or other disloyal action by any Japanese Americans. The bill promised twenty thousand dollars tax free to each prisoner of the internment camps who was alive when the bill passed. About sixty thousand former inmates of the camps were alive at that time.

The payments were scheduled to begin in October 1990, starting with the oldest survivors of the camps. Unfortunately, many did not live to see their checks arrive. With many in their seventies, eighties, and up to one hundred years old, a great number of former

The first recipients of redress checks were the oldest to be eligible for payments. The first payments were made in 1990.

inhabitants of the camps were dying with each month that it took for Congress to decide to pay the money.

When the payments finally were made, some decided to use the money for good works, like setting up scholarships. The payments brought great satisfaction to those who received the checks.[19] It meant that the government admitted that Japanese Americans had done nothing to deserve the different and undignified treatment they received during the war. More important, it meant a beginning to the end of a terrible part of their lives.

106

8

Prejudice and Discrimination in America

Fred Korematsu's attorneys made very strong arguments as his case went through the legal system. Each argument was based on the Constitution and on legal theory.

Unfortunately, Fred Korematsu's story is really about prejudice and discrimination. An entire part of this country's population was accused of being potential enemies of America, simply because of their race. Japanese Americans suffered personal loss and discrimination just because of who they were. Their rights as American citizens were denied simply because they looked different.

Does history repeat itself? The *Dred Scott* case lives in American memory as a horrible failure of white citizens to recognize the humanity of black Americans. In 1857, Chief Justice Roger Taney confirmed an American citizen's right to own slaves. Taney wrote that earlier Americans saw African slaves and their descendants as "so far inferior, that they had no rights which the white man was bound to respect."[1] Once African Americans were seen as "inferior beings," it was easy to deny them basic human rights.

Almost one hundred years after the *Dred Scott* decision, Justice Hugo Black upheld Fred Korematsu's conviction. The majority of the Court in the *Korematsu* decision "could not reject the finding of the military" that loyal Japanese Americans could not be separated from the disloyal.[2] Why were Japanese Americans as a group even suspected of disloyalty? Prejudice and discrimination against Japanese Americans because of racial differences allowed this to happen.

What is the connection between the *Dred Scott* case and the *Korematsu* decision? Japanese Americans were not labeled as "inferior beings," as African Americans had been. Still, they must have been seen as different from white Americans if their loyalty could be questioned simply because of their race.

More than fifty years have passed since the Supreme Court handed down the *Korematsu* decision. The question that remains is whether we, as Americans, have learned to push prejudice from our minds.

When the Oklahoma City Federal Building was bombed in April 1995, "fingers were raised without any basis to accuse Arabs, Muslims and Middle Easterners of being responsible for [the] crime."[3] It was such a horrible crime that many Americans did not even consider that a citizen of the United States could have been responsible. Yet two years later, a white American man was found guilty of the crime.

Although it is understandable that Americans would not want to accept the idea that a citizen of the United States could cause such a disaster in this country, it is also unfair that members of another race were immediately suspected of terrorism in Oklahoma City.

More recent history gives us another example. In 1997, President Bill Clinton formally apologized to the survivors of the Tuskegee Experiment. This experiment began in 1932 when government health researchers appeared to offer free medical treatment to African-American men who suffered from "bad blood."[4] The government knew these men had syphilis, a sexually transmitted disease. However, they did not inform the patients, or treat them for the disease, although a cure was available in the mid-1940s. The government just recorded the progress of the disease, and the effect it had on its victims.

The government paid $10 million to the survivors of the Tuskegee Experiment in 1973. However, it took almost twenty-five years longer for the government to apologize for its actions. The government, President Clinton said, "did something that was wrong—deeply . . . wrong. It was an outrage to our commitment to . . . equality for all our citizens."[5]

A 1992 Day of Remembrance exhibit included this poster commemorating the Japanese-American internment camp experience.

Japanese Americans and African Americans had to wait decades for formal apologies from their government. Because of this delay, the elderly victims of these past events did not live to hear the government apologize. After living with injustice for so long, many Japanese internees and participants of the Tuskegee Experiment died without receiving even this small satisfaction. However, these apologies may show that our nation's leaders are becoming more aware of the need to correct errors. Admitting error and accepting responsibility for the past could be an important step toward ridding America of discrimination.

Are things better today than they were during World War II? Look around your classroom and neighborhood. Are classmates from different races or religions treated differently? If they are, think about ways you could change this treatment. Perhaps you could reach out to those classmates and neighbors in a friendly way. You may be part of the effort to see that things like internment camps and unfair treatment of certain groups of people are not repeated.

Chapter Notes

Introduction

1. Quoted in Peter Irons, *Justice at War* (New York: Oxford University Press, 1983), p. 99.

2. Ibid., p. 98.

Chapter 1

1. Dillon S. Myer, *Uprooted Americans: The Japanese Americans and the War Relocation Authority during World War II* (Tucson, Ariz.: University of Arizona Press, 1971), pp. 10–11.

2. Jacobus Ten Broek et al., *Prejudice, War and the Constitution* (Los Angeles: University of California Press, 1968), p. 63.

3. Ibid., p. 189.

4. Myer, p. 12.

5. Roger Daniels, *Concentration Camps USA: Japanese Americans and World War II* (New York: Holt, Reinhart & Winston, Inc., 1972), p. 10.

6. Ibid., p. 12.

7. Quoted in John Armor and Peter Wright, *Manzanar* (New York: Times Books, 1988), pp. 27–29.

8. Daniels, p. 12.

9. Bill Hosokawa, *JACL In Search of Justice* (New York: William Morrow & Company, Inc., 1982), pp. 19–20.

10. Ibid., p. 20.

11. Gordon W. Prange, *At Dawn We Slept—The Untold Story of Pearl Harbor* (Crawfordsville, Ind.: R. R. Donnelley & Sons Co., 1982), pp. 4–5.

12. Ibid., p. 505.

13. Kenneth J. Hagan, *This People's Navy—The Making of American Sea Power* (New York: The Free Press, 1991), p. 306.

14. Prange, p. 582.

15. Quoted in William Manchester, *The Glory and the Dream* (Boston: Little, Brown and Co., 1973), p. 258.

16. *Korematsu* v. *United States*, 323 U.S. 214, 226 (1944).

17. Quoted in Martin Grodzins, *Americans Betrayed: Politics and the Japanese Evacuation* (Chicago: University of Chicago Press, 1949), p. 407.

18. Ibid.

19. Quoted in Page Smith, *Democracy On Trial: The Japanese American Evacuation and Relocation in World War II* (New York: Simon & Schuster, 1995), p. 117.

20. Ibid., pp. 120–121.

21. Ibid., p. 112.

22. Eugene V. Rostow, "The Japanese American Cases—A Disaster," *Yale Law Journal*, vol. 54, June 1945, p. 493.

23. Francis Biddle, *In Brief Authority* (Garden City, N.Y.: Doubleday & Company, Inc., 1962), p. 212.

24. Ibid., p. 213.

25. Ibid., p. 215.

26. Quoted in Armor and Wright, p. 15.

27. Ibid.

28. Ibid.

29. Biddle, p. 215.

30. Ibid., pp. 221–222.

31. Mark Jonathan Harris, Franklin D. Mitchell, and Steven J. Schecter, comps., *The Homefront: America During World War II* (New York: G. P. Putnam's Sons, 1984), p. 106.

32. Smith, pp. 126–127.

33. Myer, p. 302.

34. Ten Broek et al., p. 110.

35. Myer, p. 302.

36. Ibid., pp. 304–306.

37. Ibid., p. 302.

38. Ibid.

39. Daniels, p. 70.

40. Myer, pp. 307–308.

41. *Korematsu* v. *United States*, 323 U.S. 214, 227 (1944).

42. Myer, p. xxiv.

43. Executive Order 9066, February 19, 1942, In House Report No. 2124, 77th Cong., 2d Session., pp. 314–315.

44. Ten Broek et al., p. 120.

45. Ibid., p. 121.

46. Ibid., p. 119.

47. John Morton Blum, *Politics and American Culture During World War II* (New York: Harcourt Brace Jovanovich, 1976), pp. 160–161.

48. *Korematsu* v. *United States*, 323 U.S. 229 (1944).

49. Quoted in *Personal Justice Denied: Report of the Commission on Wartime Relocation and Internment of Civilians* (Washington, D.C.: Government Printing Office, 1982), p. 132.

50. Ibid.

51. Smith, p. 159.

52. *Personal Justice Denied*, p. 128.

53. Ibid., p. 133.

54. Quoted in John Tateishi, *And Justice for All: An Oral History of the Japanese American Detention Camps* (New York: Random House, 1984), p. 24.

Chapter 2

1. Quoted in Peter Irons, *Justice Delayed: The Record of the Japanese Internment Cases* (Middletown, Conn.: Wesleyan University Press, 1989), p. 220.

2. Mark Jonathan Harris, Franklin D. Mitchell, and Steven J. Schecter, comps., *The Homefront: America During World War II* (New York: G. P. Putnam's Sons, 1984), p. 108.

3. Eugene V. Rostow, "The Japanese American Cases—A Disaster," *Yale Law Journal*, vol. 54, June 1945, p. 502.

4. John Tateishi, *And Justice for All: An Oral History of the Japanese American Detention Camps* (New York: Random House, 1984), p. 19.

5. Jeanne Wakatsuki Houston and James D. Houston, *Farewell to Manzanar: A True Story of Japanese American Experience During and After the World War II Internment* (Boston: Houghton Mifflin, 1973), p. 19.

6. Ibid., p. 114.

7. "Gift Bears Moral for the Future," *Boston Globe*, September 11, 1988, pp. 29, 33.

8. Roger Daniels, *Concentration Camps USA: Japanese Americans and World War II* (New York: Holt, Reinhart & Winston, Inc., 1972), p. 115.

9. Ibid., 114.

10. Quoted in Irons, *Justice Delayed*, p. 133.

11. *Korematsu* v. *United States*, 323 U.S. 214, 216 (1944).

Chapter 3

1. Peter Irons, *Justice at War* (New York: Oxford University Press, 1983), p. 163.

2. Dillon S. Myer, *Uprooted Americans: The Japanese Americans and the War Relocation Authority during World War II* (Tucson, Ariz.: University of Arizona, 1971), pp. 302–303.

Chapter 4

1. Charles Lam Markmann, *The Noblest Cry: A History of the American Civil Liberties Union* (New York: St. Martin's Press, 1965), p. 3.

2. *Strauder* v. *West Virginia*, 100 U.S. 303 (1879).

3. Jacobus Ten Broek et al., *Prejudice, War and the Constitution* (Los Angeles: University of California Press, 1968), p. 113.

4. Ibid., p. 115.

5. *Korematsu* v. *United States*, 323 U.S. 214, 229 (1944).

6. Ibid., p. 216.

7. Quoted in Peter Irons, *Justice At War* (New York: Oxford University Press, 1983), p. 304.

8. Ibid.

9. *Personal Justice Denied: Report of the Commission on Wartime Relocation and Internment of Civilians* (Washington, D.C.: Government Printing Office, 1982), p. 109.

10. John Morton Blum, *Politics and American Culture During World War II* (New York: Harcourt Brace Jovanovich, 1976), p. 159.

11. *Final Report: Japanese Evacuation From the West Coast, 1942* (Washington, D.C.: Government Printing Office, 1943), p. 34.

12. Ibid.

13. Quoted in Irons, *Justice At War*, p. 306.

Chapter 5

1. *Korematsu* v. *United States*, 323 U.S. 214 (1944).

2. Ibid., p. 214.

3. Ibid., p. 219.

4. Ibid.

5. Ibid., p. 220.

6. Ibid., p. 222.

7. Ibid., p. 224.

8. Ibid.

9. Ibid.

10. Ibid., p. 225.

11. Ibid., p. 226.

12. Ibid., p. 229.

13. Ibid., p. 233.

14. Ibid., pp. 233–234.

15. Ibid., p. 234.

16. Ibid., pp. 234–235.

17. Ibid., pp. 236–237.

18. Ibid., p. 240.

19. Ibid., p. 243.

20. Ibid., pp. 243–245.

21. Ibid., p. 246.

22. Ibid., p. 247.

Chapter 6

1. Peter Irons, *Justice Delayed: The Record of the Japanese American Internment Cases* (Middletown, Conn.: Wesleyan University Press, 1989), pp. 6–7.

2. *Korematsu v. United States*, 584 F. Supp. 1406, 1412 (1984).

3. Quoted in Irons, p. 21.

4. Jacobus Ten Broek et al., *Prejudice, War and the Constitution* (Los Angeles: University of California Press, 1968), p. 96.

5. Irons, p. 139.

6. Ibid., pp. 138–139.

7. *Final Report: Japanese Evacuation From the West Coast, 1942* (Washington, D.C.: Government Printing Office, 1943), p. 9.

8. Irons, p. 128.

9. Peter Irons, *Justice At War* (New York: Oxford University Press, 1983), p. 282.

10. *Korematsu* v. *United States,* 584 F. Supp. 1406, 1412, 1413 (1984).

11. Ibid., p. 1413.

12. Ibid., p. 1420.

13. Ibid.

Chapter 7

1. Dillon S. Myer, *Uprooted Americans: The Japanese Americans and the War Relocation Authority during World War II* (Tucson, Ariz.: University of Arizona, 1971), p. 199.

2. Roger Daniels, *Prisoners Without Trial: Japanese Americans in World War II* (New York: Hill and Wang, 1993), p. 89.

3. *Personal Justice Denied: Report of the Commission on Wartime Relocation and Internment of Civilians* (Washington, D.C.: Government Printing Office, 1982), p. 118

4. Ibid., p. 120.

5. Daniels, p. 89.

6. John Armor and Peter Wright, *Manzanar* (New York: Times Books, 1988), pp. 82–83.

7. Quoted in Peter Irons, *Justice Delayed* (Middletown, Conn.: Wesleyan University Press, 1989), p. 222.

8. Daniels, p. 92.

9. Stephan Patten, "Among the Nisei Are Those Who Cannot Forget the Camps," *Baltimore Sun,* May 20, 1979, p. K4.

10. Ibid.

11. Quoted in Daniels, p. 102.

12. Patten, p. K5.

13. Daniels, p. 97.

14. Patten, p. K5.

15. Ibid.

16. Thomas E. Hitchings, ed., "War Internee Measure Enacted," *Facts on File World News Digest*, vol. 48, no. 2490, August 12, 1988, p. 594.

17. Thomas E. Hitchings, ed., "Senate Votes Internee Compensation," *Facts on File World News Digest*, vol. 48, no. 2474, April 22, 1988, p. 287.

18. Daniels, p. 103.

19. "Gift Bears Moral for the Future," *Boston Globe*, September 11, 1988, pp. 29, 33.

Chapter 8

1. Geoffrey R. Stone et al., *Constitutional Law* (Boston: Little, Brown and Company, 1986), p. 442.

2. *Korematsu* v. *United States*, 323 U.S. 214, 219 (1944).

3. *Los Angeles Times*, April 17, 1995, p. A5.

4. *The New York Times*, May 17, 1997, p. 10.

5. Ibid.

Glossary

alien—A person who is not a citizen of the country in which he or she lives.

American Civil Liberties Union (ACLU)—This organization gives legal help to those whose civil rights have been violated and who cannot afford an attorney.

amicus curiae—"Friend of the court," in Latin. A friend of the court is a person or group of people who feel they have information that should be available to the judge during a trial. These people usually have a strong opinion on the case before the court, and wish to have their views known. Friends of the court must ask permission from the judge in order to file a brief.

appeal—Asking a court with greater authority to review the decision of a lower court. There are two levels of appeal available in state and federal courts. The first is from the trial court to the intermediate court. The second is from the intermediate to the United States Supreme Court.

Bill of Rights—The first ten amendments to the United States Constitution. These amendments keep state and federal government from becoming too powerful. The Bill of Rights guarantees citizens certain rights will be protected, such as the right to free speech, freedom of religion, and freedom from unreasonable search and seizure.

certiorari—An order for a lower court to give the Supreme Court the record of a certain case. This is also used to refer to the process by which the United States Supreme Court selects the cases it will hear for review. The Supreme Court does not have to review every case brought before its attention.

concur—A concurring opinion is written by a Justice who voted with the majority in a particular case. However, that Justice may have decided as he or she did for reasons different from the others. When the Justice wishes to make that reasoning a part of the record, the information is included in a concurring opinion.

curfew—An order for a person or group of people to remain indoors for a certain part of the day for an extended period. Usually, curfews are in effect for the night, during times of war or civil unrest.

delegation—Congress can give its power to make laws to a person or group for a specific purpose. However, it must give enough guidance to that person or group so that they do not create a law that is against the Constitution.

dissent—An opinion written by one of the Justices who did not vote with the majority in a particular case. Dissenting opinions give a Justice's reasons for voting against the majority.

due process—Going through the usual processes provided by law. Due process requires that the government follow all the rules meant to protect an individual's rights. In a criminal case, the requirements of due process would include the right to a trial by jury.

equal protection—A constitutional guarantee that no person or group of people will be treated differently under the law from any other person or group of people.

error coram nobis—"The error before us," in Latin. This is a method used to ask a court to review, and to reverse, a decision made earlier in the same court. It can be used when the court made its earlier decision based on a record that included errors in the facts that were very important to the case.

espionage—Spying; giving information to another country, knowing that the information will be used to harm the defense of the United States.

evacuation—Removing people from a certain area.

exclude—To ban or keep people away from a certain place.

immigrant—A person who leaves his or her homeland to live permanently in another country.

internment—Detaining, or jailing, enemy aliens or people suspected of being disloyal.

Japanese American Citizens League (JACL)—A group made up of Japanese Americans. During World War II, this group encouraged members to cooperate with the Army in order to prove their loyalty to the country.

Justice Department—Part of the executive branch of the federal government. This department handles cases in federal matters, and interprets and enforces federal laws.

majority opinion—The written decision of a court on which the greater part of the deciding Justices agree.

nolle prosequi—"Will not further prosecute," in Latin. In a criminal matter, this is a statement by the prosecutor that has the effect of ending the legal proceedings against the defendant.

prosecutor—The person who starts a criminal proceeding against a defendant. The prosecutor also takes charge of the case and acts as the trial lawyer on behalf of the plaintiff.

reparations—Payment for a wrong suffered.

sabotage—Deliberately destroying war material or supplies necessary for national defense.

separability doctrine—Rule under which a defendant may attack only one part of a law that makes more than one demand on a person, when that person is only charged with violation of one of those demands.

"Yellow Peril"—Claim by certain people and organizations that increasing numbers of Asian immigrants in America threatened the existing lifestyle and society.

Further Reading

Biddle, Francis. *In Brief Authority*. Garden City, N.Y.: Doubleday & Company, Inc., 1962.

Blum, John Morton. *Politics and American Culture During World War II*. New York: Harcourt Brace Jovanovich, 1976.

Daniels, Roger. *Concentration Camps USA: Japanese Americans and World War II*. New York: Holt, Rinehart & Winston, Inc., 1972.

———. *Prisoners Without Trial: Japanese Americans in World War II*. New York: Hill and Wang, 1993.

Grodzins, Martin. *Americans Betrayed: Politics and the Japanese Evacuation*. Chicago: University of Chicago Press, 1949.

Harris, Mark Jonathan, Franklin D. Mitchell, and Steven J. Schecter. *The Homefront: America During World War II*. New York: G. P. Putnam's Sons, 1984.

Houston, Jeanne Wakatsuki, and James D. Houston. *Farewell to Manzanar*. New York: Bantam Books, 1973.

Irons, Peter. *Justice At War*. New York: Oxford University Press, 1983.

———. *Justice Delayed*. Middletown, Conn.: Wesleyan University Press, 1989.

Manchester, William. *The Glory and the Dream: A Narrative History of America, 1932–1972.* Boston: Little, Brown and Company, 1973.

Myer, Dillon S., *Uprooted Americans: The Japanese Americans and the War Relocation Authority during World War II.* Tucson, Ariz.: University of Arizona, 1971.

Patten, Stephan. "Among the Nisei Are Those Who Cannot Forget the Camps." *Baltimore Sun,* May 20, 1979.

Prange, Gordon. *At Dawn We Slept: The Untold Story of Pearl Harbor.* Crawfordsville, Ohio: R. R. Donnelly & Sons Company, 1982.

Rostow, Eugene. "The Japanese American Cases—A Disaster." *Yale Law Journal,* vol. 54, June 1945, p. 493.

Smith, Page. *Democracy on Trial: Japanese American Evacuation and Relocation in World War II.* New York: Simon & Schuster, 1995.

Tateishi, John. *And Justice for All: An Oral History of the Japanese American Detention Camps.* New York: Random House, 1984.

Ten Broek, Jacobus, Edward Barnhart, and Floyd Matson. *Prejudice, War and the Constitution.* Los Angeles: University of California Press, 1968.

Weglyn, Michi. *Years of Infamy.* New York: William Morrow & Co., 1976.

Index